Effects of Chiloquin Dam on Spawning Distribution and Larval Emigration of Lost River, Shortnose, and Klamath Largescale Suckers in the Williamson and Sprague Rivers, Oregon

By Barbara A. Martin, David A. Hewitt, and Craig M. Ellsworth

Prepared in cooperation with the Bureau of Reclamation

Open-File Report 2013-1039

U.S. Department of the Interior
U.S. Geological Survey

U.S. Department of the Interior
KEN SALAZAR, Secretary

U.S. Geological Survey
Suzette M. Kimball, Acting Director

U.S. Geological Survey, Reston, Virginia: 2013

For more information on the USGS—the Federal source for science about the Earth,
its natural and living resources, natural hazards, and the environment—visit
http://www.usgs.gov or call 1–888–ASK–USGS

For an overview of USGS information products, including maps, imagery, and publications,
visit *http://www.usgs.gov/pubprod*

To order this and other USGS information products, visit *http://store.usgs.gov*

Suggested citation:
Martin, B.A., Hewitt, D.A., and Ellsworth, C.M., 2013, Effects of Chiloquin Dam on spawning distribution and larval emigration of Lost River, shortnose, and Klamath largescale suckers in the Williamson and Sprague Rivers, Oregon: U.S. Geological Survey Open-File Report 2013-1039, 28 p.

Contents

Figures

Tables

Conversion Factors

SI to Inch/Pound

Multiply	By	To obtain
Length		
millimeter (mm)	0.03937	inch (in.)
meter (m)	3.281	foot (ft)
meter (m)	1.094	yard (yd)
kilometer (km)	0.6214	mile (mi)
Area		
square centimeter (cm^2)	0.001076	square foot (ft^2)
square kilometer (km^2)	247.1	acre
square kilometer (km^2)	0.3861	square mile (mi^2)
Flow rate		
cubic meter per second (m^3/s)	70.07	acre-foot per day (acre-ft/d)
cubic meter per second (m^3/s)	35.31	cubic foot per second (ft^3/s)
Mass		
gram (g)	0.03527	ounce, avoirdupois (oz)
kilogram (kg)	2.205	pound avoirdupois (lb)

Temperature in degrees Celsius (°C) may be converted to degrees Fahrenheit (°F) as follows:
°F=(1.8×°C)+32.

Effects of Chiloquin Dam on Spawning Distribution and Larval Emigration of Lost River, Shortnose, and Klamath Largescale Suckers in the Williamson and Sprague Rivers, Oregon

By Barbara A. Martin, David A. Hewitt, and Craig M. Ellsworth

Executive Summary

Chiloquin Dam was constructed in 1914 on the Sprague River near the town of Chiloquin, Oregon. The dam was identified as a barrier that potentially inhibited or prevented the upstream spawning migrations and other movements of endangered Lost River (*Deltistes luxatus*) and shortnose (*Chasmistes brevirostris*) suckers, as well as other fish species. In 2002, the Bureau of Reclamation led a working group that examined several alternatives to improve fish passage at Chiloquin Dam. Ultimately it was decided that dam removal was the best alternative and the dam was removed in the summer of 2008. The U.S. Geological Survey conducted a long-term study on the spawning ecology of Lost River, shortnose, and Klamath largescale suckers (*Catostomus snyderi*) in the Sprague and lower Williamson Rivers from 2004 to 2010. The objective of this study was to evaluate shifts in spawning distribution following the removal of Chiloquin Dam. Radio telemetry was used in conjunction with larval production data and detections of fish tagged with passive integrated transponders (PIT tags) to evaluate whether dam removal resulted in increased utilization of spawning habitat farther upstream in the Sprague River. Increased densities of drifting larvae were observed at a site in the lower Williamson River after the dam was removed, but no substantial changes occurred upstream of the former dam site. Adult spawning migrations primarily were influenced by water temperature and did not change with the removal of the dam. Emigration of larvae consistently occurred about 3–4 weeks after adults migrated into a section of river. Detections of PIT-tagged fish showed increases in the numbers of all three suckers that migrated upstream of the dam site following removal, but the increases for Lost River and shortnose suckers were relatively small compared to the total number of fish that made a spawning migration in a given season. Increases for Klamath largescale suckers were more substantial. Post-dam removal monitoring only included 2 years with below average river discharge during the spawning season; data from years with higher flows may provide a different perspective on the effects of dam removal on the spawning migrations of the two endangered sucker species.

Introduction

Dams have been used for centuries to provide benefits such as impoundments for irrigation and drinking water, flood control, and hydroelectric power. Although dams often benefit people, the cost to the environment can be variable depending on the size and type of the dam. Dams physically alter river systems and can have negative effects on some aquatic and terrestrial organisms while enhancing the populations of others (Quist and others, 2005; Hoagstrom and others, 2007). The natural process of flushing and redistribution of river sediments is interrupted by dams, often leading to altered instream habitat (Ligon and others, 1995). Generally, native fish populations are negatively affected by habitat alterations whereas exotic species may benefit (Bunn and Arthington, 2002).

Just as the early part of the 20th century was devoted to the building of dams, the last 30 years have been devoted to removing many of these aging structures. According to the U.S. Army Corps of Engineers, the 1960s was the peak of construction efforts, whereas relatively few dams have been built since the mid-1980s (Graf, 1999). Most of the dam removal efforts have focused on small headwater dams, which make up the majority of dams in the United States (Poff and Hart, 2002; Stanley and others, 2002; Doyle and others, 2005; Brenkman and others, 2012). Although it is often assumed that these small dams have minimal impacts on channel form and ecological processes, this has not always proven to be the case (Doyle and others, 2005).

The effects of dam removal can be classified into two general categories: increased connectivity and altered habitat (Doyle and others, 2005). Whereas the change in connectivity can have an immediate effect on migratory fishes, such as allowing them to pass upstream to potential spawning habitats, changes in habitat can take decades to resemble pre-dam conditions (Doyle and others, 2005). If migratory fishes encounter altered habitat upstream of the dam site, conditions may not be suitable for spawning (Kareiva and others, 2000).

Chiloquin Dam was located on the Sprague River 1.5 river kilometers (rkm) upstream of its confluence with the Williamson River and 19 rkm upstream of Upper Klamath Lake (fig. 1). The dam was constructed in 1914 to supply irrigation water for the Modoc Point Irrigation District. After its construction, the dam was fitted with three fish ladders to aid in fish passage; however, only one was functional when the dam was removed in August 2008. The functional ladder was built in 1966 and had been modified from the original pool and weir design, used for passage of salmonid populations, with baffle boards in an attempt to provide better passage for two long-lived, federally endangered catostomids, the Lost River sucker (*Deltistes luxatus*) and the shortnose sucker (*Chasmistes brevirostris*).

Limited fish passage at Chiloquin Dam was identified as one of the primary factors limiting the recovery of the populations of Lost River and shortnose suckers in Upper Klamath Lake (U.S. Fish and Wildlife Service, 2002; National Research Council, 2004; U.S. Fish and Wildlife Service, 2008). Additionally, Chiloquin Dam probably affected the migratory patterns of other fishes found in the Sprague River drainage, including Klamath largescale suckers (*Catostomus snyderi*), redband trout (*Oncorhynchus mykiss newberrii*), and several species of endemic lamprey (*Entosphenus* spp.). In 2002, the Bureau of Reclamation (Reclamation) was authorized to study the feasibility of improving fish passage at Chiloquin Dam. A technical working group was formed with representatives from Federal, State, and local agencies and organizations. The working group reached consensus that dam removal would be the best fish passage alternative. Although existing data indicated that some endangered suckers successfully negotiated the Chiloquin Dam fish ladder under certain flow conditions, the working group concluded that dam removal would improve access for all fish species in the Sprague River to upstream spawning and rearing habitat (Battelle Memorial Institute, 2005). The amount of suitable habitat and the extent to which endangered suckers would use spawning and rearing habitat upstream of the dam was largely unknown at the time of the recommendation.

The objective of this multi-year study was to evaluate shifts in spawning distribution for suckers following the removal of Chiloquin Dam. This report is a synthesis of the key findings reported in several annual reports for sucker telemetry (Ellsworth and others, 2007a, 2007b; Tyler and others, 2007; Ellsworth and VanderKooi, 2011) and larval drift (Ellsworth and others, 2008, 2009, 2011; Ellsworth and Martin, 2012). Radio telemetry was used to locate spawning areas and to determine the migration timing of spawning suckers. A series of remote detection systems for passive integrated transponder (PIT) tags installed in key locations provided supporting data on the distribution and timing of the spawning runs. Larval sampling data were used to determine shifts in spawning distribution by comparing the timing and density of larvae in the drift. We compared movement data collected before (2004–07) and after (2009–10) the removal of the dam in summer 2008 to determine whether dam removal improved sucker passage to spawning areas upstream of Chiloquin Dam.

Methods

Radio Telemetry

Fish collection, radio transmitters, and surgical procedures.—A total of 80 Klamath largescale suckers, 78 Lost River suckers, and 60 shortnose suckers were collected and fitted with transmitters at the Chiloquin Dam fish ladder during the springs of 2004–06. In addition, 159 Lost River suckers and 163 shortnose suckers collected with trammel nets in the lower Williamson River (2005 and 2007) or from the upstream trap in the Williamson River fish weir (2009 and 2010) also were fitted with transmitters. We determined the sex, spawning condition, and fork length of each fish, and then implanted a 134 kHz full-duplex PIT tag prior to the attachment of a radio transmitter. Species and sex determination for each fish was based on morphological characteristics as described in Markle and others (2005). Fish were fitted with external radio transmitters and released approximately 100 m upstream of the point of capture. We assumed, based on known life history characteristics for these and other closely related species, that upstream movement of these fish during this time of year was associated with spawning activity (Buettner and Scoppettone, 1990; Moyle, 2002). Therefore, adult size catostomids captured at the fish ladder or in the lower Williamson River in pre-spawn condition were assumed to be on an upstream spawning migration. Most fish selected for tagging were in pre-spawn condition (no expression of gametes when lightly squeezed) and had not been previously handled in USGS adult monitoring efforts as indicated by the lack of a PIT tag.

Fish were tagged and released over the duration of the spawning migrations through the Williamson River fish weir and the Chiloquin Dam fish ladder. Minimum fork length for fish selected for tagging was 350 mm. Each fish was fitted with a small external radio transmitter, Lotek MCFT-3A in 2009 and Grant Systems Engineering Pisces tags in all other years. Externally attached radio transmitters were used to minimize surgically induced stress and injury because the fish were preparing to spawn. Both types of tags had similar transmitting capabilities and size and weight characteristics. Battery life of each tag was estimated to be at least 8 to 10 weeks in all years except 2004; in 2004, battery life was estimated to be 4 to 6 weeks. Tags were programmed to transmit on up to four different frequencies ranging from 164.290 to 164.350

MHz with each tag set to generate a unique coded identifier. Field tests using these tags showed that codes could be determined at a distance of at least 100 m at ground level and 600 m from a plane flying at an altitude of 300 m.

Tagging protocols were consistent over the 6 years (2004–07 and 2009–10) except for the attachment materials used in 2004. Each fish fitted with a radio transmitter was first lightly anesthetized by placing it in a mixture of 0.1 g Tricaine Methanesulfonate (MS-222) to 1 L river water. The radio transmitters were attached externally to the fish at the dorsal fin by threading anchor material through the dorsal pterygiophores with a 15.2 mm, 14-gauge Rosenthal needle. The anchor material was passed through each fish twice for a double-posted attachment technique. Each end of the anchor material was crimped with a stainless-steel sleeve behind a 6.4-cm^2 plastic backer. In all years but 2004, the anchor material was 8.2-kg test nylon-coated, seven-strand stainless steel wire, and the nylon coating was burned off of the ends to allow a firm connection with the crimped sleeve. In early 2004, the same material was used but the coating was not burned off, which resulted in some premature tag loss because of a poor connection with the sleeve. In late 2004, 11.3-kg test monofilament was used for the anchor material as a temporary solution. Each tagged fish was allowed to recover in a holding tank with a dilute amount of StressCoat® solution for 30–60 minutes prior to being released.

Data collection.—Data for this study were collected using a combination of receivers in fixed locations as well as surveys by plane, boat, vehicle, and on foot. Our data collection strategy changed over time to increase cost-effectiveness, but changes did not compromise our ability to document spawning migrations and fish distributions (table 1). A Grant Systems Orion receiver and data logger was used at each fixed telemetry station to detect and record fish movements past the station. The reception of each receiver was tested by lowering a weighted radio transmitter to the bottom of the river at various locations near the station to ensure that a radio-tagged fish crossing in front of the station would be detected. The hardware and location of each fixed station was adjusted to maximize our ability to detect fish passing the station. Data were downloaded weekly to ensure the data loggers were working properly.

Aerial surveys were conducted on a weekly basis in a fixed-wing aircraft with a whip antenna (Model CI-177-1) attached to each wing strut of the plane. A Lotek SRX_400 receiver was used during aerial surveys to search for and locate fish with tags operating on the appropriate frequencies. Aerial surveys focused on the Williamson River up to Spring Creek at Collier Memorial State Park, the Sprague River up to the confluence of its North and South Forks, and the Sycan River up to Coyote Bucket Canyon (fig. 1). When a fish was recorded passing one of the most upstream fixed stations, the aerial survey was extended past that station and into tributaries until the fish was located or until the surveyor determined that a structure presented an instream barrier to fish movement.

Daytime ground surveys by boat, vehicle, and on foot were conducted once a week in 2004–06, and regular boat surveys were conducted twice each week in 2009 and 2010. Surveys in 2004–06 were conducted in areas where aerial surveys indicated tagged fish were concentrating, whereas surveys in 2009 and 2010 were conducted as thorough searches between the Braymill fixed telemetry station and the Williamson River fish weir (fig. 1; table 1). During the ground surveys, radio-tagged fish were located with a Lotek SRX_400 receiver and a hand-held 4-element Yagi antenna. Visual observations of suckers in the river and of fish actively spawning were noted during each survey. Locations of radio-tagged fish and observable spawning activity were recorded using a Global Positioning System unit.

Data analysis.—Migration destinations were assumed to be the farthest upstream location for each fish. Fish that moved downstream soon after tagging or remained in the general release location were assumed to be disturbed by the tagging procedure and these fish were removed from any analysis. Fish tagged from the ladder at the dam were analyzed separately from those tagged in the lower river to answer different questions. Fish tagged at the dam and released upstream of the dam were tracked to determine the farthest upstream extent of migration. The farthest upstream contacts indicated potential spawning locations upstream of the dam for fish that were helped to pass the dam. Contacts from fish tagged in the lower Williamson River were used to determine the distribution of spawning fish throughout the tributaries. Because fish collected in the lower river were tagged in 2005, 2007, 2009, and 2010, we were able to make comparisons of spawning distributions before and after dam removal.

Detections of PIT-Tagged Fish

Fish tagging and data collection.—Thousands of adult suckers were captured using various methods and in various locations from 1995 to 2010 (Hewitt and others, 2011). Each fish was scanned for the presence of a PIT tag, and when no tag was present one was inserted into the ventral musculature anterior to the pelvic girdle. From 1995 to 2004, suckers were tagged with 125 kHz full-duplex PIT tags. All tagging from 2005 to 2010 used 134 kHz full-duplex tags. Since 2005, remote antennas have been maintained at various sites along the Williamson and Sprague Rivers to detect PIT-tagged suckers throughout the spawning season (Hewitt and others, 2011).

Data analysis.—For comparison with spawning distributions inferred from relocations of fish with radio transmitters, we used detection data from remote PIT tag antennas at four locations: Williamson River at the fish weir (rkm 9.5); Sprague River upstream of Chiloquin Dam (2.5 rkm upstream of the dam); Sprague River just downstream of Chiloquin Dam (began in 2008); and Sprague River at Braymill (12 rkm upstream of the dam; began in 2009). Only 134 kHz PIT tags were included because 125 kHz tags could not be detected at all locations. We assumed that fish that migrated past the weir were on an upstream migration for spawning. For each year, we calculated the percentage of PIT-tagged suckers that passed the weir and were subsequently detected at remote antenna locations upstream. The percentages of fish that passed the weir and were later detected at the location upstream of the dam site provide an indication of the proportion of spawning fish that used spawning areas upstream of the dam site.

For comparison with larval drift data at selected sites (fig. 1 and below), we used both detection data and physical captures to illustrate the timing of upstream migration for adult female suckers in that section of the river. The first encounter of any female at each location in each spawning season was included in plots for the following locations: Williamson River fish weir (weir trap captures and remote antenna detections were compared with larval drift at the Williamson site); Chiloquin Dam site (captures in the fish ladder at the dam and remote antenna detections were compared with larval drift at the Chiloquin site); and Braymill (remote antenna detections were compared with larval drift at the Beatty site). During the high water year of 2006, the weir was not effective at capturing fish and the arrays at the weir were not always effective at detecting fish remotely; PIT tag data are more limited in that year.

Larval Drift

Data collection.—Drifting larval suckers were collected in the lower Sprague and Williamson Rivers at up to six sites from 2004 to 2010 (fig. 1). Sites were selected from available bridge crossings that facilitated sampling the river at the thalweg and provided representation of larval sucker emigration from known and suspected spawning areas. Sampling at all locations began prior to the detection of most adult suckers migrating upstream past the Williamson River fish weir or Chiloquin Dam. Sampling concluded after the number of larvae being collected had declined to just a few individuals per night and no new spawning activity had been observed for more than 4 weeks.

Drift samples were collected using plankton nets 2.5 m in length with a 0.3-m diameter circular opening supported by a stainless steel ring. Nets were constructed of 800 µm Nitex® mesh and were fitted with a removable collection cup with 500 µm Nitex® mesh windows. A General Oceanics Model 2030R flowmeter with a standard rotor was used to record water velocities at the mouth of the net at sites where water velocities were great enough to keep the net suspended in the water column. At sites where water velocities were not great enough to keep the net suspended in the water column, the net was modified with a PVC hoop fixed to the net opening and a polystyrene float fixed to the collection cup to keep the net horizontal in the water column and to keep the net from collapsing around the flow meter. A General Oceanics Model 2030R6 flowmeter with a low-velocity rotor was used to record water velocities at these sites. A 6-mm rope was attached to one side of the stainless steel ring at the opening of the net for deployment and retrieval from bridges. A pancake-shaped weight (either 3.6 or 4.5 kg depending on water velocity) was attached to the opposite side of the ring to hold the net opening perpendicular to the river flow. Drift samples were collected in the thalweg for 10 minutes from the downstream side of each bridge. Start and end times and flowmeter readings were recorded in the field for each sample. We collected drift samples three times a week on Sunday, Tuesday, and Thursday nights. Samples were collected at all sites from sunset to between 5 and 8.25 hours after sunset at 0.5–2.0 hour intervals. The sampling interval was determined primarily by travel time between sites because a single technician was responsible for samples at two sites each night.

Following the retrieval of a drift net, any larvae, eggs, or debris impinged on the sides of the net were rinsed into the collection cup. All material was then transferred into sample bottles and fixed in 10 percent formalin. Fish specimens and eggs were sorted from sample debris within 24 hours of collection. Fish specimens were enumerated, stored in 95 percent ethanol, and delivered to Oregon State University (2004–08) or kept at USGS (2009–10) for identification and measurement. Larvae were identified under magnification (2–10x) to the lowest possible taxonomic level using a key for larval fishes of the Upper Klamath Basin (Oregon State University, unpub. data, 2004). Larval sucker species identification was based primarily on differences in pigmentation (dorsal melanophores), which generally allows for separation of Lost River sucker larvae from shortnose and Klamath largescale sucker larvae. Because the pigmentation patterns between shortnose suckers and Klamath largescale suckers are similar, we were unable to positively identify larvae of either of these species; therefore, larvae identified as either shortnose suckers or Klamath largescale suckers were combined and designated as shortnose/Klamath largescale for this report. Larval suckers exhibiting intermediate characteristics used to separate Lost River sucker larvae from shortnose/Klamath largescale larvae were designated as unidentified sucker larvae. Larvae that were damaged to the point where identification could not be made also were designated as unidentified sucker larvae.

Data analysis.—The occurrence and density of sucker larvae and eggs in the drift were compared across years in relation to patterns in the timing of adult sucker migrations, water temperature, and river discharge. For summary statistics in plots and tables, the time period included for each species at each site in each season began when larvae were first captured and ended on the date when the last capture occurred. Nightly densities for the plots were calculated as the total number of Lost River or shortnose/Klamath largescale sucker larvae captured divided by the total volume of water sampled in a night. To compare the general magnitude of drifting larvae among sites and years, we used the median of the non-zero density values as a measure of central tendency. Zero observations complicate simple summary statistics, but the frequency of zero observations can provide information about differences among sites and years. Therefore, we also report the percentage of zero observations at each site in each year. In all plots and summaries, densities of larvae in the drift illustrate the timing of larval emigration. Densities provide only coarse indications of differences in magnitude among sites and years because they are not corrected for differences in hydraulic conditions among sites or variation in discharge within and among seasons. Water temperature and discharge data were obtained from the Sprague River gage at rkm 8.7 (U.S. Geological Survey stream gage 11501000) and from the Williamson River gage at rkm 16.6 downstream of the confluence with the Sprague River (U.S. Geological Survey stream gage 11502500).

Results

Spawning Locations Upstream of the Dam Site

Suckers radio-tagged and released above the dam (2004–06) showed different likelihoods, depending on species, to travel upstream of their release point. Across the 3 years, 66 percent of the Klamath largescale suckers, 55 percent of the Lost River suckers, and 37 percent of the shortnose suckers captured at the dam migrated upstream of the release location in the impoundment above the dam (table 2). Of the fish that migrated upstream of the impoundment, the majority of Klamath largescale suckers migrated to Beatty Gap or one of the tributaries near Beatty Gap. A large percentage of radio-tagged shortnose suckers were never contacted upstream of the release site (44–79 percent), and of those that were only one (in 2005) migrated upstream of the Chiloquin Narrows (fig. 1). Lost River suckers appeared to use more locations upstream of the dam than shortnose suckers, with 18–47 percent of the upstream migrants going to Beatty Gap or one of the tributaries near Beatty Gap. In contrast to shortnose suckers, 29–78 percent of the Lost River suckers that migrated upstream of the release site went above the Chiloquin Narrows.

Adult Sucker Spawning Migrations and Distribution

For suckers radio-tagged and released in the Williamson River, 42–100 percent of Lost River suckers and 3–14 percent of shortnose suckers were detected in the Sprague River in a given year (table 3). The vast majority of shortnose suckers stopped somewhere between the weir on the Williamson River and the confluence with the Sprague River, and no shortnose suckers passed the dam site in any year. In all years but 2005, the farthest upstream contact for many of the shortnose suckers was at the weir site, and the fate of these individuals is uncertain (table 3). No Lost River suckers passed the dam site prior to dam removal, but two Lost River suckers (3 percent) passed upstream of the dam site in 2009 and 7 (11 percent) did so in 2010.

Only three of the radio-tagged Lost River suckers (all from 2010) migrated upstream beyond the upper end of the section of the Sprague River that was impounded prior to dam removal. Klamath largescale suckers were only radio-tagged in the Williamson River in 2005, and only eight fish were tagged. None of these fish were detected in the Sprague River and only one was detected upstream of the weir in the Williamson River (Ellsworth and others, 2007a).

Remote PIT tag antennas continuously detected PIT-tagged suckers throughout the spawning seasons in which they were operational. The number of Lost River and shortnose suckers detected on the antennas generally increased through time as more individuals in the populations were tagged (table 4). For Klamath largescale suckers, most individuals were tagged during sampling in the fish ladder at Chiloquin Dam. Once the dam was removed, the number of Klamath largescale suckers detected on the remote antennas declined as mortality or movement out of the area was not balanced by new tags being put out at other locations. The proportion of Klamath largescale suckers that passed the weir and were subsequently detected on antennas upstream of the dam site was higher than for either Lost River or shortnose suckers (table 4). Furthermore, the proportion of Klamath largescale suckers that migrated upstream of the dam site increased greatly after dam removal to more than 45 percent in each year. The increase in the number of Klamath largescale suckers detected at Braymill relative to the antennas at and upstream of the dam site is due to the greater detection efficiency at the Braymill site. In contrast to the other river-wide arrays where the antennas lay on the river bottom (pass over), the antennas at Braymill stand up (pass through) in a narrower channel. Nonetheless, the numbers show that the vast majority of PIT-tagged Klamath largescale suckers that migrate to the dam site continue on into the upper Sprague River. Overall, more than 57 percent of the Klamath largescale suckers that passed the weir migrated to Braymill upstream of the Chiloquin Narrows in each year after dam removal.

A higher percentage of Lost River suckers (28–32 percent) than shortnose suckers (11–16 percent) that passed the weir were subsequently detected on the PIT tag antennas located just downstream of the dam site (table 4). However, more of the shortnose suckers that migrated to the antennas downstream of the dam site continued on upstream of the dam site, such that the overall percentage of fish that migrated from the weir to the site upstream of the dam was similar between the two species. Although only a small percentage of either of the endangered species migrated to the antennas upstream of the dam site (≤ 7 percent), the percentage did increase for both species in the years following dam removal. Less than 1 percent of the Lost River and shortnose suckers that passed the weir in any year passed the remote antennas at Braymill, indicating that most of the endangered suckers that passed the dam site did not migrate much farther upstream. The PIT tag detections show that it is not the same Lost River and shortnose suckers passing the Braymill antennas each year. In both 2010 and 2011, more than 50 percent of the Lost River suckers detected at Braymill had not been detected there previously. The limited data on shortnose suckers showed that all 7 fish that passed Braymill in 2010 had passed those antennas in a previous year, whereas none of the 14 fish that passed Braymill in 2011 had done so previously.

Larval Sucker Emigration

Larval drift samples were collected at up to six locations during the study. In general, sucker larvae were collected in the highest densities at the Williamson site, followed by the Chiloquin and Beatty sites (table 5). Sampling at the sites between Chiloquin and Beatty—Power Station, Lone Pine, and Sycan—generally yielded few or no sucker larvae and are not discussed further. We observed an increase in the densities of drifting larvae over time at the Williamson site, particularly in the 2 years following dam removal. The greatest annual median density of larvae at the Williamson site occurred in 2010 for Lost River suckers and 2009 for shortnose/Klamath largescale suckers. In contrast, larval densities were lower and generally similar through time at the Chiloquin and Beatty sites, and no increases in density were apparent in the years following dam removal (table 5). We did note that the annual median densities for Lost River sucker larvae were highest at the Beatty and Sycan sites in 2006 (table 5), a year with particularly high river discharge during the spawning season (fig. 2).

Compared to densities of larvae in the drift, the density of sucker eggs was much lower and without pattern at sites other than the Chiloquin site. The Chiloquin site was located just downstream of a known spawning area between the confluence of the Williamson and Sprague Rivers and the dam site (because of this proximity, larval drift occurred earlier in the night at this site as well; Ellsworth and Martin, 2012). We observed a substantial three- to four-fold increase in the density of drifting eggs at the Chiloquin site in 2009, the year following dam removal. Egg densities in 2010 at this site were similar to densities in 2007 and 2008 prior to dam removal. The lowest egg densities were observed in 2006, the year with high river discharge.

We examined the timing of spawning migrations for PIT-tagged adult female suckers in each year to compare with the timing of larval drift. Based on the first encounters of individuals in a given season, the timing of the migrations varied among years primarily due to differences in water temperature. Klamath largescale suckers always migrated first, followed by Lost River suckers and then shortnose suckers (figs. 3–6). Klamath largescale suckers began their spawning run when water temperatures were about 8°C, whereas Lost River suckers began their spawning runs at 10°C and shortnose suckers began their spawning runs at 12°C. Lost River and shortnose suckers appeared to spawn between the beginning of April and the end of June, with the majority spawning mid-April to mid-May, while Klamath largescale suckers could start moving upstream as early as February.

At the Williamson and Chiloquin sites, Lost River sucker larvae generally were captured in May and early June, earlier than shortnose/Klamath largescale sucker larvae (figs. 3–6). The separation was most pronounced at the Chiloquin site. Although the shortnose/Klamath largescale sucker larvae at the Williamson and Chiloquin sites may be a mix of the two species, the larvae appear to follow the migration of adult female shortnose suckers and we concluded that they are predominantly shortnose sucker larvae. Larval drift at Beatty occurred a month earlier than at the Williamson and Chiloquin sites, typically ending by late May or early June (figs. 7 and 8). Timing of emigration for Lost River sucker larvae and shortnose/Klamath largescale sucker larvae generally was similar at the Beatty site, with a more protracted drift period compared to the Williamson and Chiloquin sites. The emigration of Lost River sucker larvae at the Beatty site also was most protracted in 2006, a year with particularly high discharge (fig. 7). The timing of drift for shortnose/Klamath largescale sucker larvae at Beatty appeared to follow the migration of adult female Klamath largescale suckers past the Braymill PIT tag antennas (fig. 8). Combined with the fact that few PIT-tagged shortnose suckers were detected at the Braymill antennas, we concluded that the larvae collected at Beatty were Klamath largescale suckers. In general, larval suckers were collected in the drift at a site about 3–4 weeks after adult females migrated into that section of the river, with the delay for shortnose suckers being somewhat longer than for Lost River suckers. A stark exception to this pattern was the timing of larval drift for Lost River suckers at Beatty, where larvae were collected in the drift during the same time period when PIT-tagged females were detected at the Braymill antennas about 100 rkm downstream (fig. 7).

Discussion

Although it was hypothesized that Lost River suckers and shortnose suckers would utilize more spawning areas upstream of Chiloquin Dam once it was removed, PIT tag data showed only a small increase in the percentage of individuals passing the dam site in the 2 years after removal. The information from radio-tagged fish corroborated the PIT tag findings that the vast majority of endangered suckers did not migrate upstream beyond the former impoundment area above the dam site. Furthermore, larval sampling did not show any substantial changes in the densities of drifting larvae among sites upstream of the dam after removal. However, we did observe increased larval densities at the Williamson site, well downstream of the former dam in the 2 years following dam removal. We do not know whether the increased larval densities at this site were associated with the removal of the dam. Throughout the study, the majority of larvae were collected at the Williamson site, followed by the Chiloquin and Beatty sites. This larval drift pattern supports the conclusion that the majority of Lost River and shortnose suckers continued to spawn downstream of the former dam site.

Prior to the removal of Chiloquin Dam, a lake wide telemetry study showed only one Lost River sucker (3 percent) and one shortnose sucker (2 percent) fitted with internal transmitters to have passed upstream of the Chiloquin Dam (Banish and others, 2007). Similarly, in this study, none of the radio-tagged Lost River or shortnose suckers passed upstream of the dam prior to dam removal. After dam removal, only three Lost River suckers migrated upstream of the former impoundment above the dam site, and none of them reached the Chiloquin Narrows. We conclude that most of the increase in spawning of endangered suckers upstream of the dam site following dam removal was restricted to the river section downstream of Chiloquin Narrows, and this is supported by PIT tag detection data showing that the vast majority of PIT-tagged individuals that passed the former dam site were not detected at the next upstream antennas at Braymill. We anticipated that the small contingent of endangered suckers that did migrate upstream of Braymill would be composed of the same individuals each year, but PIT tag data did not support this idea. Although Klamath largescale suckers appeared to spawn primarily in the upper reaches of the Sprague River, the vast majority of Lost River and shortnose suckers spawned in the Williamson River and the Sprague River downstream of the dam site.

Our study did not find any substantial increases in habitat use by Lost River or shortnose suckers upstream of the dam site following dam removal, but we only monitored sucker movements and larval drift for 2 years after the dam was removed. Other dam removal studies have shown that sometimes decades are required for restoration of habitat and ecological functions after dam removal (Feld and others, 2011; Helms and others, 2011), although some systems stabilize within a few years (Kanehl and others, 1997; Catalano and others, 2007). Catalano and others (2007) speculated that short-term studies after dam removal do not necessarily show changes in spawning behavior of long-lived species with slow rates of population increase. Consequently, changes in spawning behavior for Lost River and shortnose suckers in the Williamson and Sprague Rivers may not be detected for many years. Furthermore, river flows were relatively low in the two study years that followed dam removal (2009 and 2010), so results from those years may not be representative of potential future habitat use. Burdick and Hightower (2006) found that use of upstream habitats by anadromous fishes following dam removal was dependent on river flow. Similarly, we observed increased larval densities of Lost River suckers at the Beatty and Sycan sites in 2006, a particularly high water year, and adult sucker monitoring efforts found a substantial increase in the number of Lost River suckers at the Chiloquin Dam in that year (Hewitt and others, 2011). Although Lost River suckers appeared to migrate farther upstream in the high water year of 2006, shortnose suckers did not show the same trend. This indicates that shortnose suckers may prefer to spawn in the lower river while Lost River suckers will take the opportunity to spawn farther upstream when flow conditions allow.

Although the amount of time required for the restoration of ecological function after dam removal is often dependent on the size and function of the dam, another key issue is the amount of sediment that was retained by the dam. Doyle and others (2005) indicated that geomorphic response, such as the effects of sediment deposition, should be most noticed directly adjacent to the dam site, with effects decreasing exponentially with both distance and time. Thomson and others (2005) concluded that ecological restoration was dependent on the rate of transport of fine sediment downstream, which depends on the amount of sediment initially impounded by the dam and flow conditions after dam removal. The Chiloquin Dam was a low-head irrigation diversion structure estimated to have 45,000 cubic yards of sediment trapped in the impoundment upstream of the dam (Battelle Memorial Institute 2005). Doyle and others (2003) noted that once sediment is transported downstream, the magnitude and duration of its effects can vary greatly. Removal of other small low-head dams has often led to short-term problems associated with increased sedimentation that often stabilize after about a year (Shuman, 1995; Stanley and others, 2002; Ahearn and Dahlgren, 2005; Helms and others, 2011). Such increased sedimentation would support our observation of increased sucker egg drift at the Chiloquin site in 2009, the first year after dam removal. Although we observed increased armoring of the substrate downstream of the dam site after dam removal (B. Hayes, USGS, oral communication, 2012), we did not quantify the size of the sediments and therefore do not know the amount of fine sediments in the interstitial spaces in the gravel at the spawning areas in 2009 or 2010. The substrate appeared to remain armored through the 2010 spawning season, but densities of drifting sucker eggs did not continue to be elevated in that year. Thus, factors other than sedimentation may have contributed to the higher densities of drifting sucker eggs downstream of the dam site in 2009.

With the exception of Lost River suckers at Beatty, our study found that larval drift of all three suckers occurred about 3–4 weeks after adult suckers migrated into a section of river. The June sucker (*Chasmistes liorus*), another endangered lakesucker, has shown a similar time frame of about 3 weeks from spawning to larval drift (Modde and Muirhead, 1994; U.S. Fish and Wildlife Service, 1999). The timing of larval drift for Lost River suckers at Beatty is a strong exception to the general pattern observed at the other sites. Adult female Lost River suckers with PIT tags were detected migrating past antennas at Braymill at the same time that larvae were drifting at the Beatty site, about 100 rkm upstream. Furthermore, the production of Lost River sucker larvae at this site is substantial and comparable in some years to densities observed at the Chiloquin site. This suggests that the vast majority of Lost River suckers spawning upstream of the Beatty site have not been tagged. There are two possible explanations for this scenario, and they are not necessarily mutually exclusive. Lost River suckers that spawn at Beatty may be a unique contingent of the population that migrates before our sampling efforts begin. We consider this to be unlikely as the sole explanation because our adult sampling often started in mid-February. Because larvae generally were first detected at Beatty in late March or early April, we would expect that our sampling and the upstream migration of fish that produced those larvae would have overlapped to some extent. Although Perkins and others (2000) mentioned an early migrating contingent of Lost River suckers, their data were similar to what we observed in 2006 when a few Lost River suckers began their migration as early as mid-March. The other explanation is that Lost River suckers that spawn at Beatty are resident in the upper Sprague River and have therefore never been available to our sampling program. Anecdotal evidence exists to support this explanation and future efforts to PIT tag spawning adults in the upper Sprague River may be worthwhile. For example, Larry Dunsmoor of the Klamath Tribes observed Lost River suckers spawning at Kirk Spring in the upper Sprague River in the third week of March in 1995 (Perkins and others, 2000). This coincides with when we would expect Lost River suckers to spawn at Beatty to produce drifting larvae in April and May. It also is possible that Lost River suckers spawning upstream of the Beatty site are a combination of migrants from Upper Klamath Lake and residents in the upper Sprague River. The pattern of larval drift in some years (for example, 2006, 2010) appears to be bimodal and larvae drifting at Beatty late in the season may be migrants from Upper Klamath Lake.

We found that the timing of sucker spawning migrations was linked to increasing water temperatures and that each species began migration at a slightly different temperature, consistent with studies on other *Catostomus* species (Dence, 1948; Brown and Graham, 1954; Geen and others, 1966; Corbett and Powles, 1983; Modde and Muirhead, 1994). Throughout our study, Klamath largescale suckers began migration before Lost River and shortnose suckers and went the farthest upstream. After the removal of Chiloquin Dam, there was a substantial increase in the number of Klamath largescale suckers migrating upstream past the former dam site. Lost River suckers migrated next and used more spawning habitat upstream of the location of Chiloquin Dam than shortnose suckers. For the two endangered species, increases in the use of spawning habitat upstream of the dam site after removal were far less than we observed for Klamath largescale suckers, and appeared to be restricted to the section of river downstream of Chiloquin Narrows. Nonetheless, removal of Chiloquin Dam restored connectivity with potential spawning habitat upstream. Future monitoring, particularly in years with high river flows, could determine whether the endangered suckers make use of this habitat.

Acknowledgments

We thank personnel from the U.S. Geological Survey Klamath Falls Field Station for assistance with collecting and processing field data and for reviewing and editing drafts of this report. We also thank Doug Markle, Dave Simon, and other Oregon State University staff for processing laboratory data from 2004 to 2008. This report was funded by the Bureau of Reclamation, U.S. Department of Interior (Interagency Agreement 07AA200144), and the U.S. Geological Survey. Funding was provided by Reclamation as part of its mission to manage, develop, and protect water and related resources in an environmentally and economically sound manner in the interest of the American public. Fish samples were obtained under Endangered Species permit TE-007907 issued by the U.S. Fish and Wildlife Service and under various scientific taking permits issued by the Oregon Department of Fish and Wildlife.

References Cited

Ahearn, D.S., and Dahlgren, R.A., 2005, Sediment and nutrient dynamics following a low-head dam removal at Murphy Creek, California: Limnology and Oceanography, v. 50, p.1752-1762.

Banish, N.P., Adams, B.J., and Shively, R.S., 2007, Distribution and habitat associations of radio-tagged adult Lost River and shortnose suckers in Upper Klamath Lake, Oregon, 2005-2006: Report to Bureau of Reclamation, 42 p., Contract #02AA200099 and #06AA204053.

Battelle Memorial Institute, 2005, Environmental assessment for the Chiloquin Dam Fish Passage Project: Prepared by Battelle Memorial Institute for the Bureau of Indian Affairs, Northwest Regional Office, Portland, Oregon, 97 p. + appendices.

Brenkman, S.J., Duda, J.J., Torgersen, C.E., Welty, E., Pess, G.R., Peters, R., and McHenry, M.L., 2012, A riverscape perspective of Pacific salmonids and aquatic habitats prior to large-scale dam removal in the Elwha River, Washington, USA: Fisheries Management and Ecology, v. 19, p. 36-53.

Brown, C.J.D., and Graham, R.J., 1954, Observations on the longnose sucker in Yellowstone Lake: Transactions of the American Fisheries Society, v. 83, p. 38-46.

Buettner, M., and Scoppettone, G., 1990, Life history and status of catostomids in Upper Klamath Lake, Oregon: U.S. Fish and Wildlife Service completion report, 108 p.

Bunn, S.E., and Arthington, A.H., 2002, Basic principles and ecological consequences of altered flow regimes for aquatic biodiversity: Environmental Management, v. 30, p. 492-507.

Burdick, S.M., and Hightower, J.E., 2006, Distribution of spawning activity by anadromous fishes in an Atlantic slope drainage after removal of a low-head dam: Transactions of the American Fisheries Society, v. 135, p. 1290-1300.

Catalano, M.J., Bozek, M.A., and Pellett, T.D., 2007, Effects of dam removal on fish assemblage structure and spatial distributions in the Baraboo River, Wisconsin: North American Journal of Fisheries Management, v. 27, p. 519-530.

Corbett, B., and Powles, P.M., 1983, Spawning and early-life ecological phases of the white sucker in Jack Lake, Ontario: Transactions of the American Fisheries Society, v. 112, p. 308-313.

Dence, W.A., 1948, Life history, ecology and habits of the dwarf sucker, *Catostomus commersonnii utawana* Mather, at the Huntington Wildlife Station: Roosevelt Wildlife Bulletin, v. 8, p. 82-150.

Doyle, M.W., Stanley, E.H., and Harbor, J.M., 2003, Channel adjustments following two dam removals in Wisconsin: Water Resources Research, v. 39, p. ESG 2—1-15.

Doyle, M.W., Stanley, E.H., Orr, C.H., Selle, A.R., Sethi, S.A., and Harbor, J.M., 2005, Stream ecosystem response to small dam removal: lessons from the heartland: Geomorphology, v. 71, p. 227-244.

Ellsworth, C.M., Banks, D.T., and VanderKooi, S.P., 2011, Patterns of larval sucker emigration from the Sprague and lower Williamson Rivers of the Upper Klamath Basin, Oregon, prior to the removal of Chiloquin Dam—2007/2008 annual report: U.S. Geological Survey Open-File Report 2011-1108, 30 p.

Ellsworth, C.M., Luton, C.D., Tyler, T.J., VanderKooi, S.P., and Shively, R.S., 2007a, Spawning migration movements of Klamath largescale, Lost River, and shortnose suckers in the Williamson and Sprague Rivers, Oregon, prior to the removal of Chiloquin Dam—annual report 2006: Report to Bureau of Reclamation, 51 p.

Ellsworth, C.M., and Martin, B.A., 2012, Patterns of larval sucker emigration from the Sprague and lower Williamson Rivers of the Upper Klamath Basin, Oregon, after the removal of Chiloquin Dam—2009/2010 annual report: U.S. Geological Survey Open-File Report 2012-1037, 34 p.

Ellsworth, C.M., Tyler, T.J., Luton, C.D., VanderKooi, S.P., and Shively, R.S., 2007b, Spawning migration movements of Klamath largescale, Lost River, shortnose suckers in the Williamson and Sprague Rivers, Oregon prior to the removal of Chiloquin Dam—annual report 2005: Report to Bureau of Reclamation, 42 p.

Ellsworth, C.M., Tyler, T.J., VanderKooi, S.P., and Markle, D.F., 2008, Patterns of larval catostomid emigration from the Sprague and lower Williamson Rivers of the Upper Klamath Basin, Oregon, prior to the removal of Chiloquin Dam—2004–2005 annual report: Report to Bureau of Reclamation, 45 p.

Ellsworth, C.M., Tyler, T.J., VanderKooi, S.P., and Markle, D.F., 2009, Patterns of larval sucker emigration from the Sprague and lower Williamson Rivers of the Upper Klamath Basin, Oregon, prior to the removal of Chiloquin Dam—2006 annual report: U.S. Geological Survey Open-File Report 2009-1027, 32 p.

Ellsworth, C.M., and VanderKooi S.P., 2011, Spawning migration movements of Lost River and shortnose suckers in the Williamson and Sprague Rivers, Oregon, following the removal of Chiloquin Dam—2009 Annual Report: U.S. Geological Survey Open-File Report 2011-1147, 20 p.

Feld, C.K., Birk, S., Bradley, D.C., Hering, D., Kail, J., Marzin, A., Melcher, A., Nemitz, D., Pedersen, M.L., Pletterbauer, F., Pont, D., Verdonschot, P.F.M., and Friberg, N., 2011, From natural to degraded rivers and back again: a test of restoration ecology theory and practice, in Woodward, G., ed., Advances in Ecological Research, v. 44:, p. 119-209.

Geen, G.H., Northcote, T.G., Hartman, G.F., and Lindsey, C.C., 1966, Life histories of two species of catostomid fishes in Sixteenmile Lake, British Columbia, with particular reference to inlet stream spawning: Journal of the Fisheries Research Board of Canada, v. 23, p. 1761-1788.

Graf, W.L., 1999, Dam nation: a geographic census of American dams and their large-scale hydrologic impacts: Water Resources Research, v. 35, p. 1305-1311.

Helms, B.S., Werneke, D.C., Gangloff, M.M., Hartfield, E.E., and Feminella, J.W., 2011, The influence of low-head dams on fish assemblages in streams across Alabama: Journal of the North American Benthological Society, v. 30, p. 1095-1106.

Hewitt, D.A., Hayes, B.S., Janney, E.C., Harris, A.C., Koller, J.P., and Johnson, M.A., 2011, Demographics and run timing of adult Lost River (*Deltistes luxatus*) and shortnose (*Chasmistes brevirostris*) suckers in Upper Klamath Lake, Oregon, 2009: U.S. Geological Survey Open-File Report 2011-1088, 24 p.

Hoagstrom, C.W., DeWitte, A.C., Gosch, N.J.C., and Berry, C.R., JR., 2007, Historical fish assemblage flux in the Cheyenne River below Angostura Dam: Journal of Freshwater Ecology, v. 22, p. 219-229.

Kanehl, P.D., Lyons, J., and Nelson, J.E., 1997, Changes in the habitat and fish community of the Milwaukee River, Wisconsin, following removal of the Woolen Mills Dam: North American Journal of Fisheries Management, v. 17, p. 387-400.

Kareiva, P., Marvier, M., and McClure, M., 2000, Recovery and management options for spring/summer Chinook salmon in the Columbia River Basin: Science, v. 290, p. 977-979.

Ligon, F.K., Dietrich, W.E., and Trush, W.J., 1995, Downstream ecological effects of dams, a geomorphic perspective: BioScience, v. 45, p. 183-192.

Markle, D.F., Cavalluzzi, M.R., and Simon, D.C., 2005, Morphology and taxonomy of Klamath Basin suckers (Catostomidae): Western North American Naturalist, v. 65, p. 473-489.

Modde, T., and Muirhead, N., 1994, Spawning chronology and larval emergence of June sucker (*Chasmistes liorus*): Great Basin Naturalist, v. 54, p. 366-370.

Moyle, P.B., 2002, Inland fishes of California: Berkeley and Los Angeles, California, University of California Press, 502 p.

National Research Council, 2004, Endangered and threatened fishes in the Klamath River Basin: causes of decline and strategies for recovery: The National Academics Press, Washington, DC, 398 p.

Perkins, D.L., Scoppettone, G.G., and Buettner, M., 2000, Reproductive biology and demographics of endangered Lost River and shortnose suckers in Upper Klamath Lake, Oregon: Report to Bureau of Reclamation, 40 p.

Poff, N.L., and Hart, D.D., 2002, How dams vary and why it matters for the emerging science of dam removal: BioScience, v. 52, p. 659-668.

Quist, M.C., Hubert, W.A., and Rahel, F.J., 2005. Fish assemblage structure following impoundment of a Great Plains river: Western North American Naturalist, v. 65, p. 53-63.

Shuman, J.R., 1995, Environmental considerations for assessing dam removal alterations for river restoration: Regulated Rivers: Research and Management, v. 11, p. 249-261.

Stanley, E.H., Luebke, M.A., Doyle, M.W., and Marshall, D.W., 2002, Short-term changes in channel form and macroinvertebrate communities following low-head dam removal: Journal of the North American Benthological Society, v. 21, p. 172-187.

Thomson, J.R., Hart, D.D., Charles, D.F., Nightengale, T.L., and Winter, D.M., 2005, Effects of removal of a small dam on downstream macroinvertebrate and algal assemblages in a Pennsylvania stream: Journal of the North American Benthological Society, v. 24, p. 192-207.

Tyler, T.J., Ellsworth, C.M., VanderKooi, S.P., and Shively, R.S., 2007, Riverine movements of adult Lost River, shortnose, and Klamath largescale suckers in the Williamson and Sprague Rivers, Oregon—Annual Report 2004: Report to Bureau of Reclamation, 29 p.

U.S. Fish and Wildlife Service, 1999, June sucker (*Chasmistes liorus*) Recovery Plan: U.S. Fish and Wildlife Service, Denver, Colorado, 61 p.

U.S. Fish and Wildlife Service, 2002, Biological/conference opinion regarding the effects of operation of the Bureau of Reclamation Project on the endangered Lost River sucker (*Deltistes luxatus*), shortnose sucker (*Chasmistes brevirostris*), threatened Bald Eagle (*Haliaeetus leucocephalus*), and proposed critical habitat for the Lost River/shortnose suckers for June 1, 2002 – March 31, 2012: Klamath Falls, Oregon.

U.S. Fish and Wildlife Service, 2008, Biological/conference opinion regarding the effects of the Bureau of Reclamation's proposed 10-year operation plan (April 1, 2008–March 31, 2018) for the Klamath Project and its effects on the endangered Lost River and shortnose suckers: Klamath Falls Fish and Wildlife Office, Klamath Falls, Oregon and Yreka Fish and Wildlife Office, Yreka, California, 197 p. + appendices.

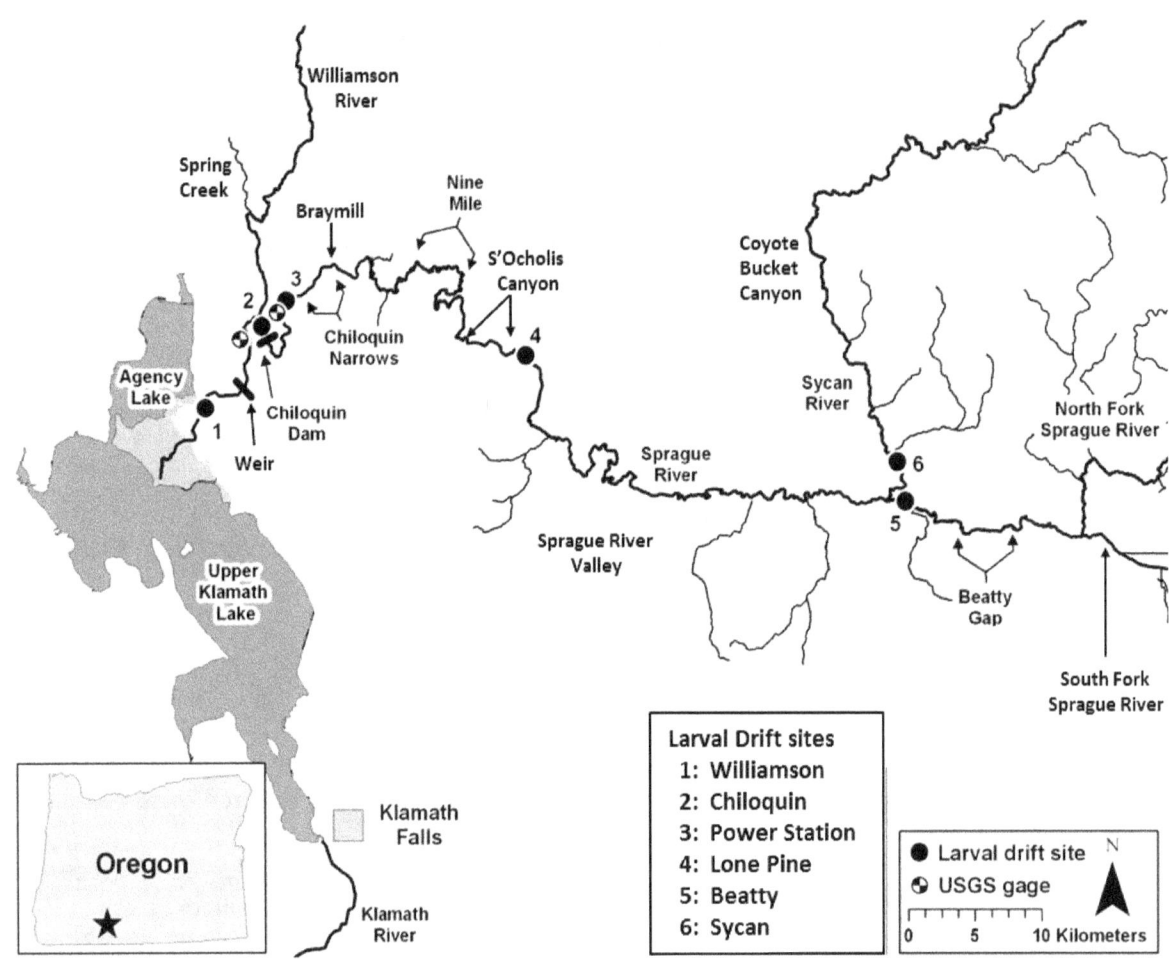

Figure 1. Map of study area showing larval drift sampling sites and areas where adult suckers were located with telemetry and remote PIT tag antennas. Specific locations for the larval drift sites were bridges at (1) rkm 7.7 on the Williamson River (Williamson); (2) rkm 0.8 on the Sprague River (Chiloquin); (3) rkm 9.1 on the Sprague River (Power Station); (4) rkm 52.5 on the Sprague River (Lone Pine); (5) rkm 108 on the Sprague River (Beatty); and (6) rkm 4.7 on the Sycan River (Sycan).

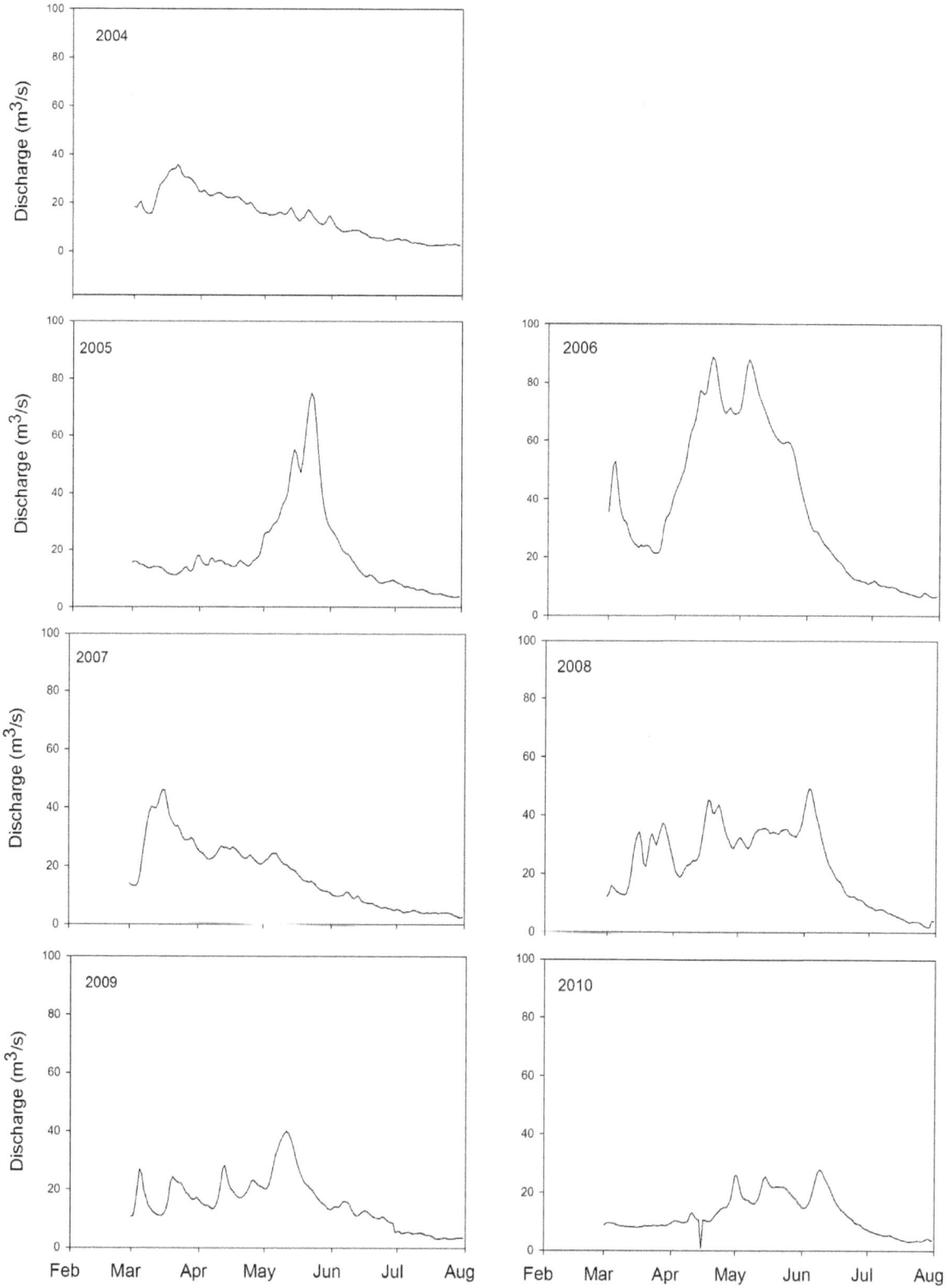

Figure 2. River discharge from the USGS gage on the lower Sprague River (11501000).

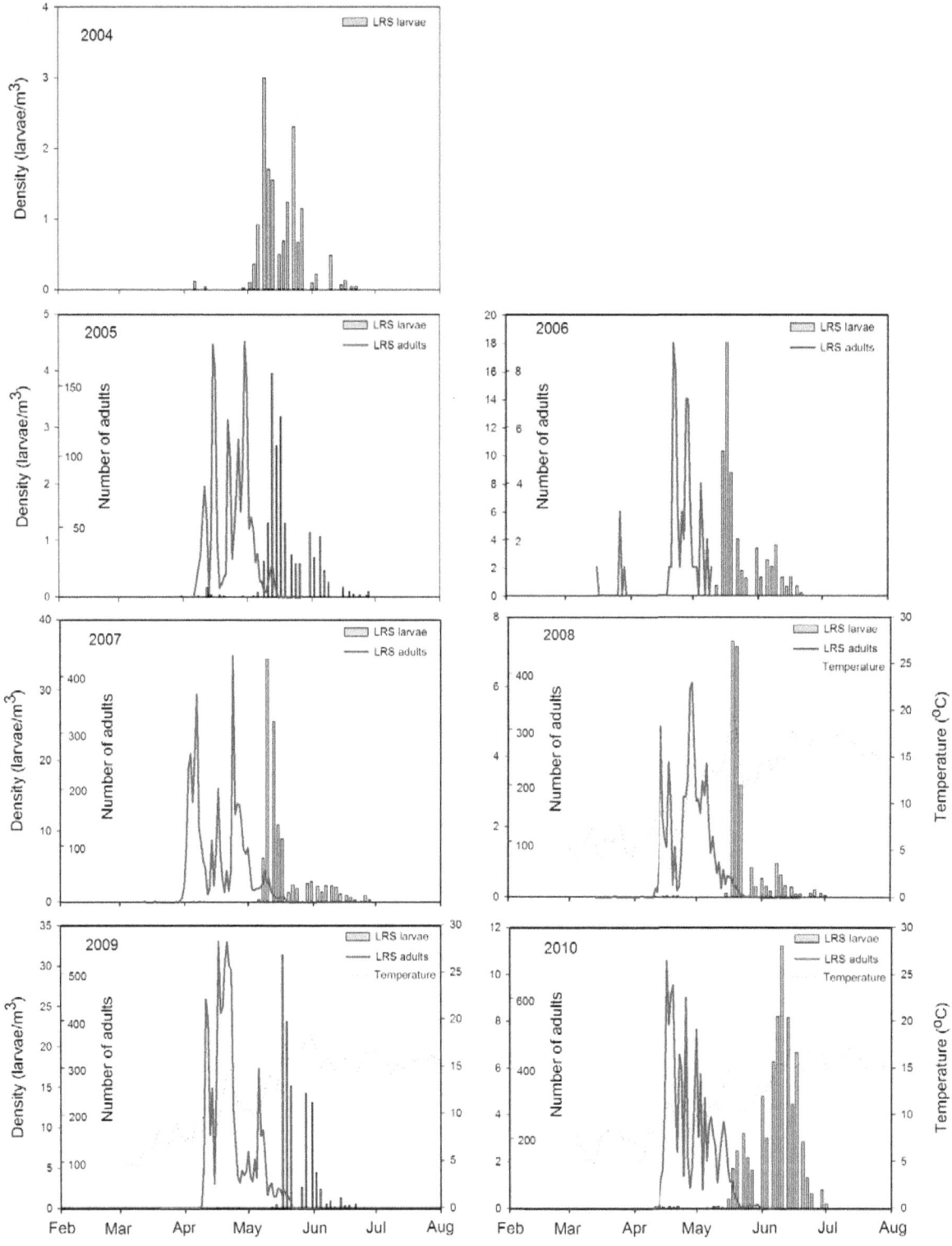

Figure 3. Timing of spawning migrations for PIT-tagged adult female Lost River suckers at the Williamson River weir and observed nightly densities of Lost River sucker larvae in the drift at the Williamson site. Water temperature is from the USGS gage on the Williamson River downstream of the confluence with the Sprague River (11502500).

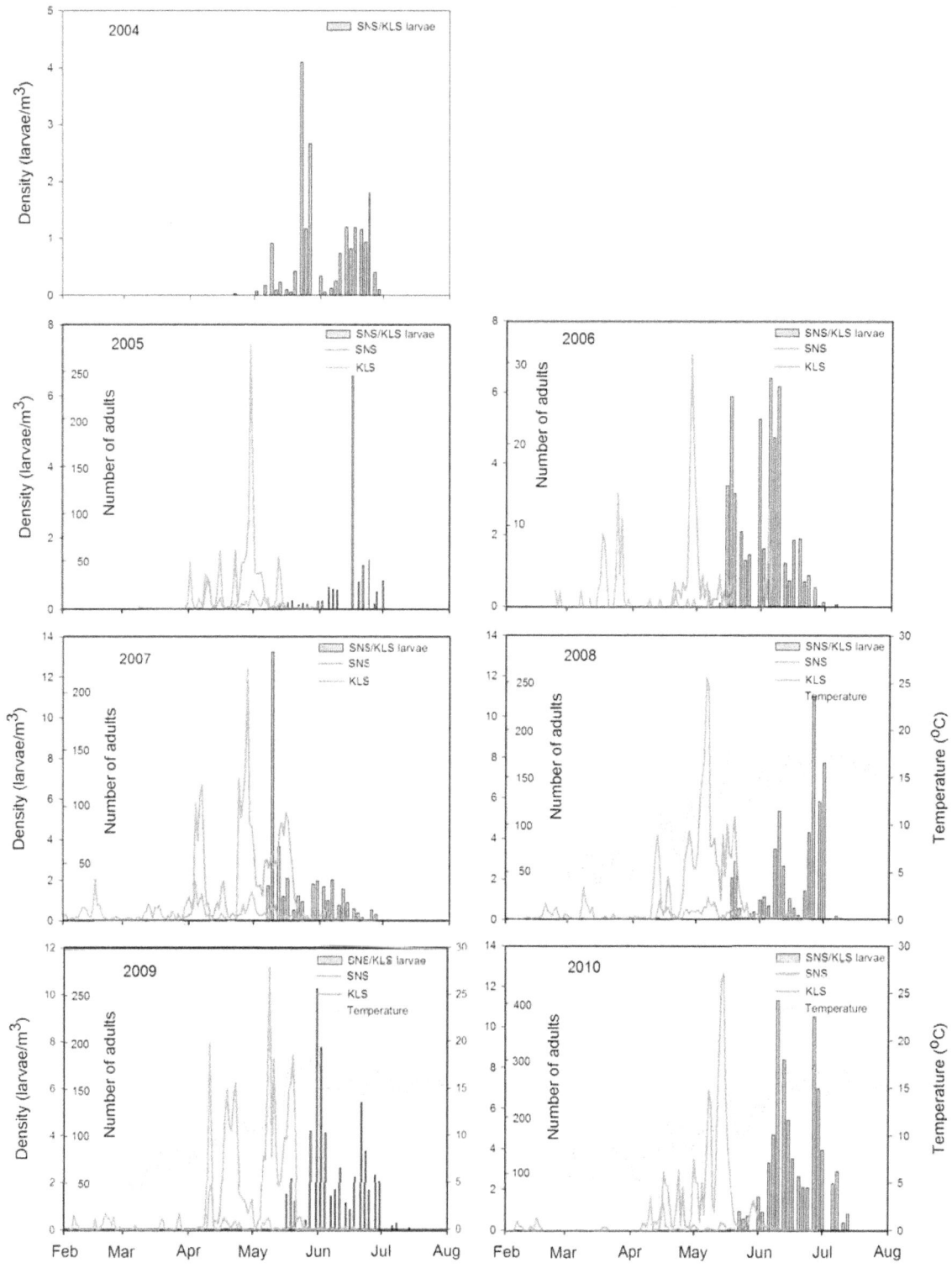

Figure 4. Timing of spawning migrations for PIT-tagged adult female shortnose and Klamath largescale suckers at the Williamson River weir and observed nightly densities of shortnose/Klamath largescale sucker larvae in the drift at the Williamson site. Water temperature is from the USGS gage on the Williamson River downstream of the confluence with the Sprague River (11502500).

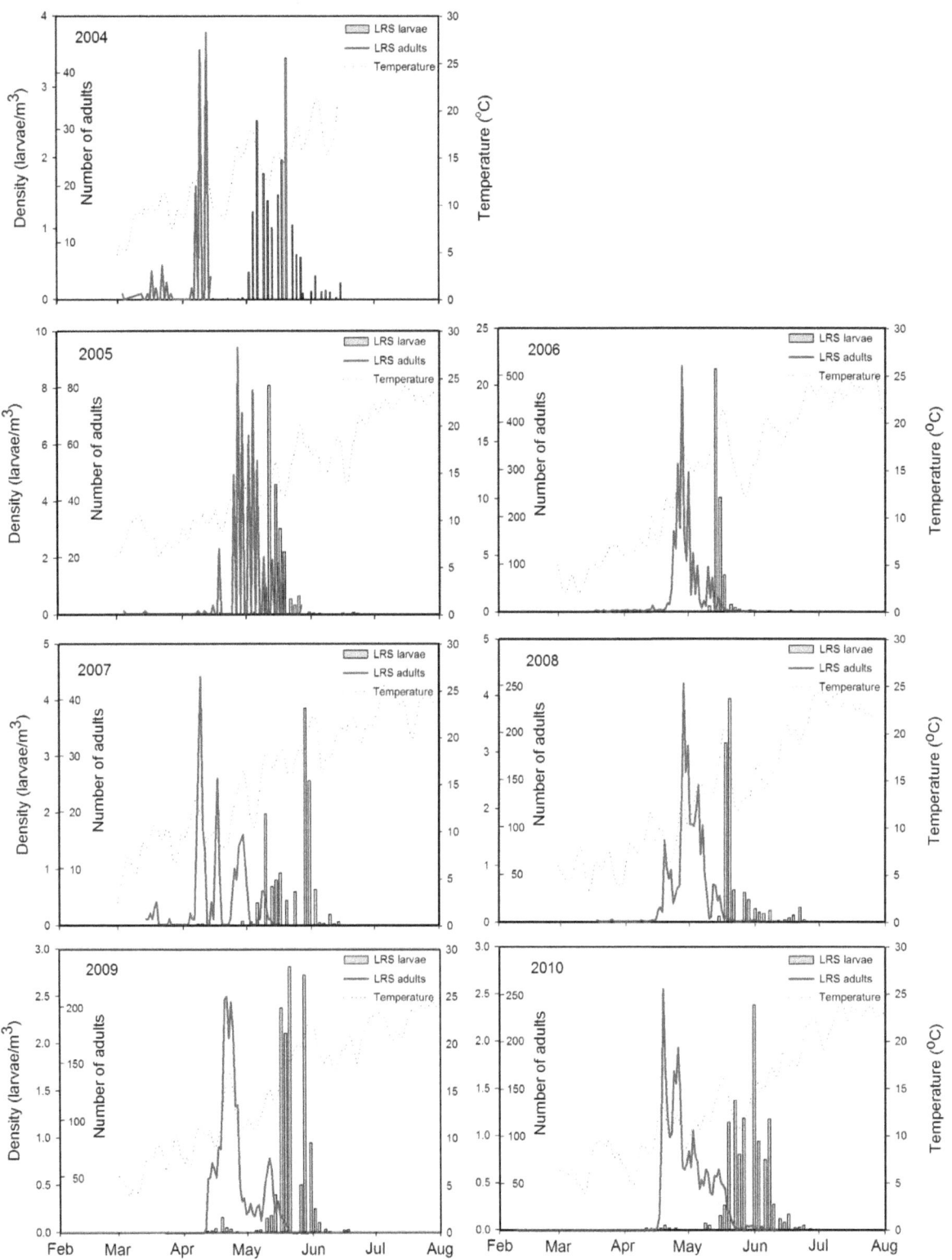

Figure 5. Timing of spawning migrations for PIT-tagged adult female Lost River suckers at the Chiloquin Dam site and observed nightly densities of Lost River sucker larvae in the drift at the Chiloquin site. Water temperature is from the USGS gage on the lower Sprague River (11501000).

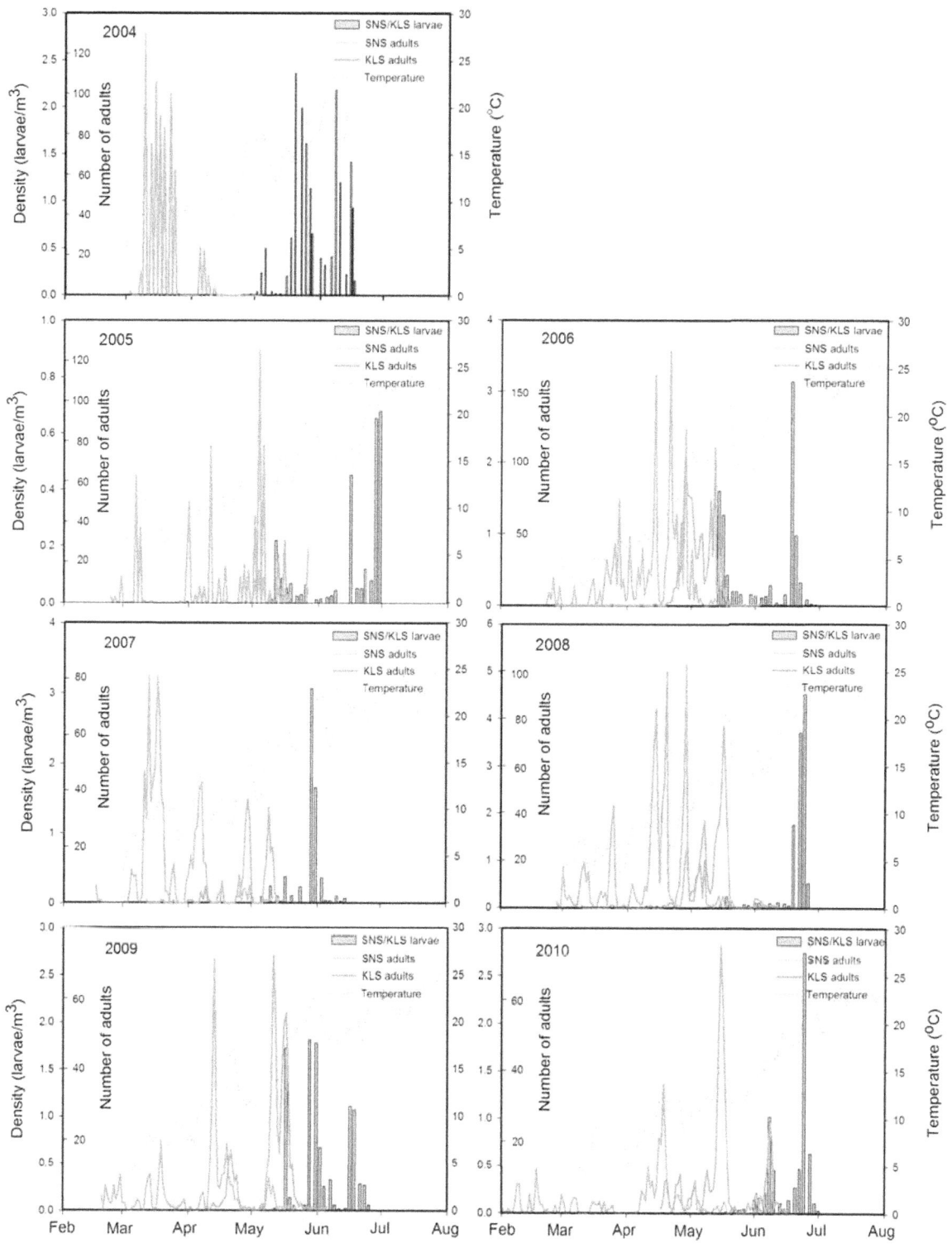

Figure 6. Timing of spawning migrations for PIT-tagged adult female shortnose and Klamath largescale suckers at the Chiloquin Dam site and observed nightly densities of shortnose/Klamath largescale sucker larvae in the drift at the Chiloquin site. Water temperature is from the USGS gage on the lower Sprague River (11501000).

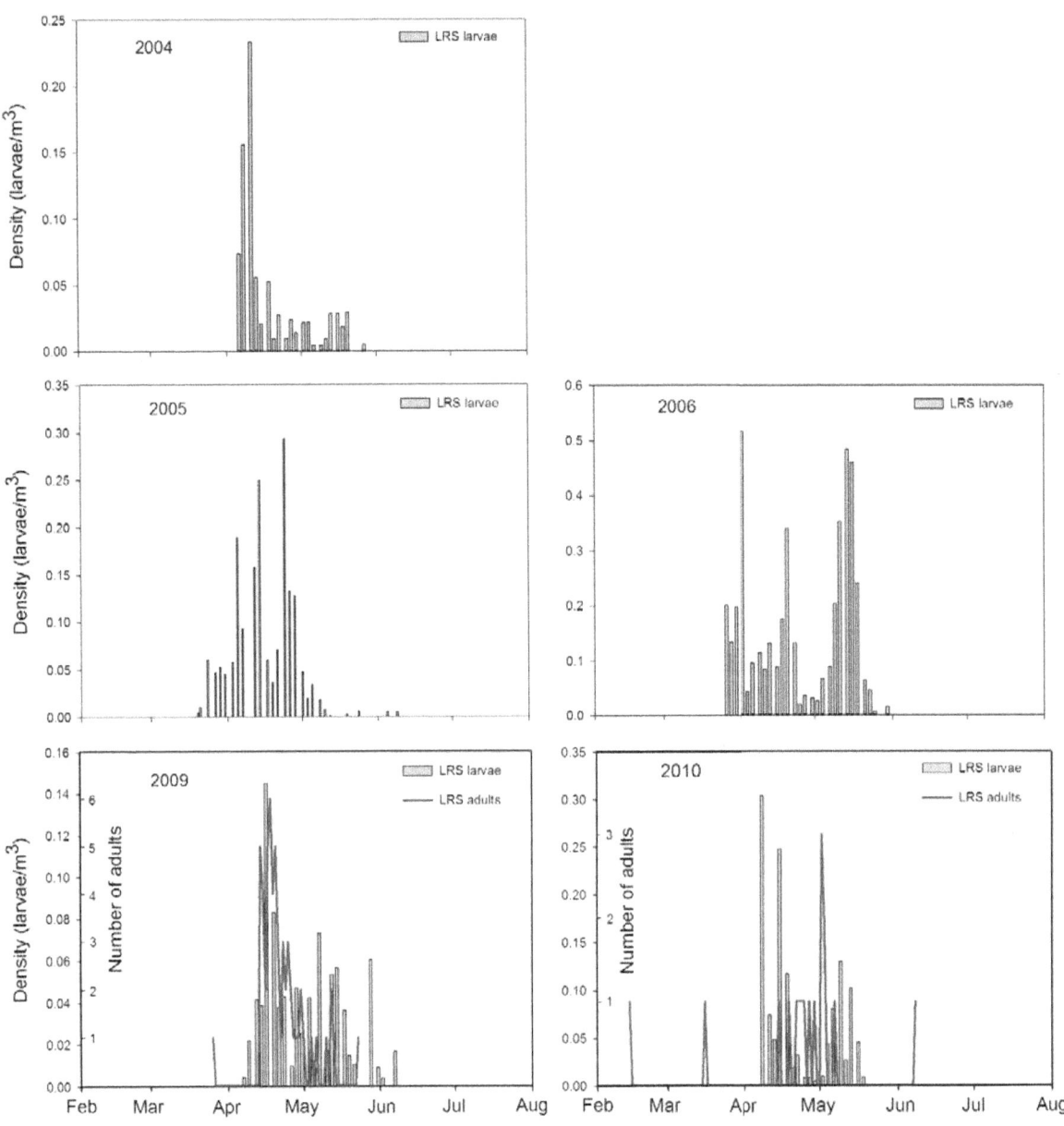

Figure 7. Timing of spawning migrations for PIT-tagged adult female Lost River suckers at Braymill and observed nightly densities of Lost River sucker larvae in the drift at the Beatty site.

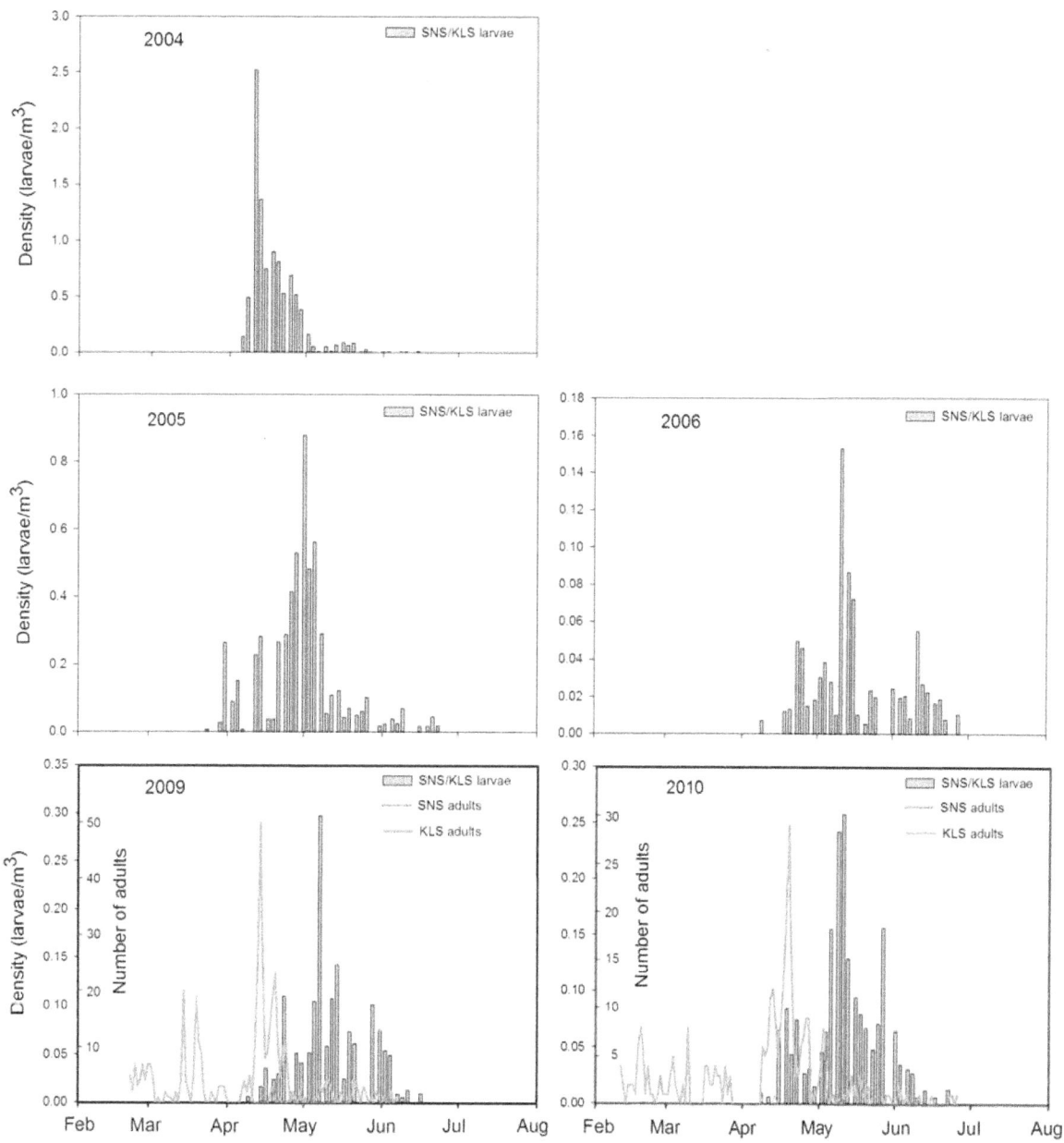

Figure 8. Timing of spawning migrations for PIT-tagged adult female shortnose and Klamath largescale suckers at Braymill and observed nightly densities of shortnose/Klamath largescale sucker larvae in the drift at the Beatty site.

Table 1. Radio telemetry data collection during pre-dam removal (2004–07) and post-dam removal periods (2009 and 2010) of the study.

[The bottom section of the table indicates the locations that were used for the fixed receivers in the different years. Upstream distances for the fixed receivers are measured from Upper Klamath Lake; the confluence of the Williamson and Sprague Rivers is at rkm 17.6. Although larval drift sampling was conducted in 2008, the year in which Chiloquin Dam was removed, no telemetry was conducted in that year]

	Pre-dam removal				Post-dam removal	
	2004	2005	2006	2007	2009	2010
Ground surveys (boat, vehicle, on foot)	X	X	X		X	X
Aerial surveys	X	X	X			
Fixed location receivers		X	X	X	X	X
Locations of fixed receivers						
Lake (Williamson River at rkm 0)		X	X	X		
River Bend (Williamson River at rkm 4.5)					X	X
Weir (Williamson River at rkm 9.5)		X	X	X	X	X
Chiloquin (Sprague River at rkm 18)			X	X	X	X
Chiloquin Dam (Sprague River at rkm 19)			X	X	X	X
Braymill (Sprague River at rkm 31)		X	X		X	X
S'Ocholis Canyon (Sprague River at rkm 64.7)		X	X		X	X
Sycan River (Sycan River at rkm 126)			X		X	X
Lower Beatty Gap (Sprague River at rkm 129)		X	X		X	X
Upper Beatty Gap (Sprague River at rkm 135)		X			X	X

Table 2. Farthest upstream contact of Klamath largescale suckers, Lost River suckers, and shortnose suckers fitted with radio transmitters and released in the impoundment upstream of Chiloquin Dam, 2004–06.

[River kilometers (rkm) start at the confluence of Upper Klamath Lake and the Williamson River and continue upstream along the Sprague River corridor; rkm 17.6 is at the confluence of the Williamson and Sprague Rivers and Chiloquin Dam was at rkm 19. Individuals that moved downstream after tagging or remained near their release site in the impoundment upstream of the dam were removed from further analysis]

Area	rkm	Klamath largescale suckers			Lost River suckers			shortnose suckers		
		2004 (n=25)	2005 (n=27)	2006 (n=28)	2004 (n=20)	2005 (n=26)	2006 (n=32)	2004 (n=9)	2005 (n=23)	2006 (n=28)
Sycan River		0	1	1	0	0	1	0	0	0
North Fork Sprague River		0	2	2	0	0	0	0	0	0
Beatty Gap	129.1–137.7	5	12	10	4	3	7	0	0	0
Sprague River Valley	69.9–129.0	0	0	0	1	0	1	0	0	0
S'Ocholis Canyon	64.8–69.8	0	0	3	0	0	0	0	0	0
Nine Mile Area	30.7–64.7	1	3	4	2	2	3	0	1	0
Chiloquin Narrows	27.8–30.6	0	1	0	0	3	2	0	0	1
Power Station[a]	19.6–27.7	4	2	2	2	9	3	5	10	5
Removed from analysis										
Impoundment above Dam	19.0–19.5	10[b]	2	2	6[b]	2	6	2	2	3
Upper Williamson to Lower Sprague Rivers	9.5–18.9	1	1	3	2	7	9	0	9	16
Lower Williamson River (below weir) to Upper Klamath Lake	0–9.4	3	0	0	1	0	0	0	0	2
No detection after release		1	3	0	2	0	0	2	1	1

[a] Includes many fish that migrated only a kilometer or less upstream of the impoundment, particularly for LRS and SNS in 2005.

[b] Some fish were always recorded near their release location, and were suspected to have shed transmitters due to the use of nylon-coated wire for attachment.

25

Table 3. Farthest upstream contact of Lost River suckers and shortnose suckers fitted with radio transmitters and released in the lower Williamson River (2005 and 2007) or upstream of the Williamson River fish weir (2009 and 2010).

[River kilometers (rkm) start at the confluence of Upper Klamath Lake and the Williamson River and continue upstream along the Sprague River corridor; rkm 17.6 is at the confluence of the Williamson and Sprague Rivers and Chiloquin Dam was at rkm 19. Individuals that moved downstream after tagging or were not detected after their release were removed from further analysis. Individuals with a farthest upstream contact in the Williamson River at the site of the weir in 2009 and 2010. We do not know whether noted in parentheses. The fate of these individuals is uncertain, particularly for fish released upstream of the weir in 2009 and 2010. We do not know whether these fish migrated above that point between surveys or stayed in that area suffering from the effects of capture and transmitter attachment; it is possible that they did not spawn that year]

Area	rkm	Lost River suckers				Shortnose suckers			
		2005 (n=33)	2007 (n=4)	2009 (n=58)	2010 (n=64)	2005 (n=36)	2007 (n=26)	2009 (n=56)	2010 (n=45)
Upstream of the Chiloquin Dam impoundment	19.6-22.5[b]	0	0	0	3	0	0	0	0
Impoundment above Chiloquin Dam[a]	19.0-19.5	0	0	2	4	0	0	0	0
Lower Sprague River to Chiloquin Dam	17.7-18.9	11	3	27	24	1	3	3	1
Upper Williamson River to Sprague River	9.5-17.6	6 (0)	0	27 (2)	33 (12)	13 (3)	17 (17)	52 (17)	30 (18)
Lower Williamson River (below weir) to Upper Klamath Lake	0-9.4	9	0	2	0	11	1	1	4
Removed from analysis									
Downstream to Upper Klamath Lake		3	0	0	0	6	1	0	0
No detection after release		4	1	0	0	5	4	0	10[c]

[a] This section was free flowing in 2009 and 2010.

[b] The fish that moved farthest upstream was a Lost River sucker female in 2010; her migration apparently ended downstream of Chiloquin Narrows.

[c] Three of these transmitters appeared to fail very soon after the fish were released.

Table 4. Number of suckers with 134 kHz PIT tags that passed the antennas at the Williamson River fish weir (rkm 9.5) and were then subsequently detected upstream somewhere in the Sprague River (downstream of the dam site = rkm 19, upstream of the dam site = rkm 21.7, Braymill = rkm 31).

	Weir	Downstream of the dam site	Upstream of the dam site	Braymill	Percentage upstream of the dam site
Lost River sucker					
2007	5,683	--	5	--	0.1
2008	6,843	2,011	12	--	0.2
2009	10,807	3,419	764	71	7.1
2010	13,651	3,834	543	17	4.0
2011	15,234	4,280	800	59	5.3
Shortnose sucker					
2007	2,892	--	12	--	0.4
2008	3,474	552	63	--	1.8
2009	4,178	574	289	10	6.9
2010	5,724	645	341	7	6.0
2011	4,833	609	336	13	6.9
Klamath largescale sucker					
2007	773	--	27	--	3.5
2008	903	770	51	--	5.6
2009	934	595	500	641	53.5
2010	703	391	385	420	54.8
2011	569	341	256	329	45.0

27

Table 5. Annual median densities of Lost River sucker larvae and shortnose/Klamath largescale sucker larvae among sampling sites in the Williamson and Sprague Rivers before and after removal of Chiloquin Dam in summer 2008.

[Sampling locations are shown in figure 1. Annual median densities were based on all non-zero nightly densities between the first and last capture of larvae of a given species in a season. The number of non-zero samples for a season is given in parentheses and the percentage of samples with no larvae are given below]

Species Sampling site	Density of sucker larvae (larvae/m³)						
	2004	2005	2006	2007	2008	2009	2010
Lost River sucker:							
Sycan			0.02 (12) 96%			0.00 (0) 100%	0.00 (0) 100%
Beatty	0.03 (59) 67%	0.07 (106) 68%	0.15 (100) 60%			0.05 (94) 70%	0.08 (67) 79%
Lone Pine	0.04 (10) 92%	0.03 (16) 93%	0.02 (40) 81%			0.06 (47) 72%	0.05 (8) 95%
Power Station	0.03 (14) 89%	0.04 (18) 92%	0.02 (34) 83%	0.03 (38) 93%	0.02 (23) 94%	0.03 (17) 93%	0.06 (6) 97%
Chiloquin	0.36 (104) 38%	0.10 (177) 50%	0.06 (200) 50%	0.10 (266) 51%	0.11 (197) 55%	0.14 (173) 58%	0.12 (219) 48%
Williamson	0.58 (73) 61%	0.54 (183) 61%	0.97 (176) 56%	1.25 (265) 50%	0.46 (155) 69%	1.97 (109) 71%	2.19 (129) 66%
shortnose/Klamath largescale sucker:							
Sycan			0.02 (28) 91%			0.07 (46) 86%	0.05 (39) 88%
Beatty	0.20 (113) 37%	0.12 (177) 47%	0.05 (71) 72%			0.08 (111) 65%	0.08 (138) 57%
Lone Pine	0.03 (19) 85%	0.03 (3) 99%	0.02 (7) 97%			0.03 (24) 86%	0.03 (3) 98%
Power Station	0.04 (3) 98%	0.03 (4) 98%	0.02 (4) 98%	0.03 (19) 96%	0.02 (25) 94%	0.05 (3) 99%	0.03 (1) 100%
Chiloquin	0.28 (103) 39%	0.06 (118) 67%	0.19 (131) 68%	0.06 (185) 66%	0.07 (227) 48%	0.17 (119) 71%	0.07 (161) 62%
Williamson	0.63 (92) 51%	0.26 (161) 65%	1.47 (148) 63%	0.90 (198) 63%	1.19 (225) 55%	3.04 (124) 67%	2.70 (139) 63%

www.ingramcontent.com/pod-product-compliance
Lightning Source LLC
Chambersburg PA
CBHW080354290526
45791CB00009BA/2874